You Can't Save Us

What Survivors Actually Need from the People
Around Them

Melody C. Gross

CS Publishing

Book Cover by Marcus Kiser
Author Photo by Alvin C. Jacobs, Jr.

Contents

To the dedicated advocates, activists, community organizers, supporters and movement makers.
Thank you!

Introduction

In July of 2025, I finished writing my first book, "No One's Coming to Save You." My goal for that book was to provide survivors of intimate partner violence with strategies and tools for navigating life after abuse. I began planning the marketing of the book, which included a book tour and a release event. When I was asked who would be invited to the release event, my initial response was survivors and those working in the gender-based violence movement. When asked the same question by a potential sponsor, I hesitated and realized I may want to expand my invite list. But that made me question what I have to offer those outside of the previous two groups. Although I make mention of other groups and speak about them on social media and in my writing, I knew that wasn't going to be enough. That led me to write, "You Can't Save Us: What Survivors Actually Need from the People Around Them."

Before you delve into this book, I want you to hold fast to one truth: *Relationship abuse impacts every aspect of our lives.*

Again, *relationship abuse impacts every aspect of our lives.*

Last time, *relationship abuse impacts every aspect of our lives.*

Now you said it three times, so you can't forget or deny it.

"You Can't Save Us" is divided into four groups: family, friends, neighbors, and employers. In each of those groups, I'll share how the relationship abuse impacts it, how you can support survivors, and how that leads to the disruption of domestic violence. Disrupting domestic violence takes three components: awareness, belonging, and change. Awareness + Belonging + Change = Disruption. A + B + C = D. After each chapter, there is a section that answers some of the most frequently asked questions related to that chapter. Consider this section a quick Q&A. I'll delve into the ABCs of disruption shortly, but first, a note about those who harm. After each chapter, there is a section that answers some of the most frequently asked questions related to that chapter. Consider this section a quick Q&A.

Those who harm

Unfortunately, the eradication of domestic violence can not occur without the transformation of those who are abusive. There are few programs and outdated models to support individuals who have harmed others. Often, these programs are voluntary and lack cultural responsiveness. That is not a judgment of those doing the work with people who abuse. Instead, I want us to find ways to advocate for more responses to domestic violence that involve engaging abusive people beyond the criminal system. Domestic violence is viewed as a learned behavior. You learn to be either a victim or a perpetrator. Those who harm must discover ways to address their violence and abuse.

What you need to know about domestic violence

Do you cringe when you hear someone say "domestic violence?" When speaking with people about my work, they will either whisper "domestic violence" or try their best to avoid saying it at all. I get it. It makes people uncomfortable. It should. It should never be something we are comfortable with. Being comfortable can lead to being complacent. Sometimes to make people feel more at ease, I'll use the term "relationship abuse," which tends to be much more receptive. Throughout this book, you'll notice I say "relationship abuse," but I'll also use "intimate partner violence." While domestic violence encompasses relationships between two people, it can also refer to relatives (parent/child, grandmother/grandson, cousins). Other terms you may have heard include dating violence, domestic abuse, interpersonal relationship abuse, spousal abuse, family violence, or dating abuse. For the sake of clarity, when I use domestic violence, I am referring to two people who are or have previously been in an intimate relationship.

But what is domestic violence? If you search for the definition of domestic violence, you'll notice many different ones. Any number of organizations may have other definitions, along with the legal definition that impacts laws and legislation. To ensure continuity, I will refer to the Office on Violence Against Women's definition as "a **pattern** of abusive behavior in any relationship that is used by one partner to gain or maintain **power and control** over another intimate partner. Domestic violence can be physical, sexual, emotional, economic, psychological, or technological actions or threats of actions or other patterns of coercive behavior that influence another person within an intimate partner relationship. This includes any behaviors that intimidate, manipulate, humiliate, isolate, frighten, terrorize, coerce, threaten, blame, hurt, injure, or wound someone." Those are a lot of words, so I want you to focus on three words: pattern, power, and control. If you don't remember anything else (although I hope you do), remember that domestic violence is a pattern of power and control over another person.

Within that definition, you also see the types and tactics of abuse that take place. To give you a better understanding, I want to provide you with some examples of each type so you can have a grasp on what your family member, friend, neighbor, or colleague may endure. Additionally, my work is from a place of empowerment; therefore, I will rarely use the term "victim" to describe someone experiencing relationship abuse but instead refer to them as a "**survivor.**" That is an initial act to give them back their power and autonomy.

Types and Tactics of Abuse

- Economic/financial abuse. They don't allow the survivor to work, take their paycheck, or stop them from pursuing their education.

- Coercive control. Intimidate the survivor into doing something they otherwise would not do.

- Isolation. Threats, manipulation, coercion, or physical violence keep the survivor away from their family and friends.

- Physical abuse. Biting, pinching, kicking, slapping,

punching, strangling, throwing objects, driving recklessly, using weapons, or forcing or denying food.

- Emotional abuse. Name-calling, insults, possessiveness, untrustworthiness, humiliation, blame, denying or minimizing the abuse, threats, yelling, cheating, accusing the survivor of cheating, or criticism.

- Stalking. Showing up at the survivor's workplace without consent.

- Spiritual abuse. Weaponizing religious scripture to control the survivor.

- Sexual abuse. Force, threats, or manipulation to engage in sexual activities.

- Abuse by immigration status. Threaten to contact government entities to disrupt immigration proceedings.

- Abuse by gender or sexual identity. Threatening to "out" the survivor to family, friends, or employer.

- Legal abuse. Filing repeated petitions or motions, or false charges.

- Reproductive abuse. Forcing the survivor to get an abortion or use birth control.

- Digital/Technological abuse. Logging into the survivor's social media accounts without consent.

Relationship abuse is much more prevalent than people think. I could provide you with a bunch of data to support my claims. But what you should never forget is that **someone you know is or has experienced some form of relationship abuse.** While you can't save everyone, even those closest to you, you can take action and learn what survivors actually need from the people around them. And, I'm here to help you do it.

The ABCs of Disruption

Domestic violence only ends when those who abuse receive the tools they need to end the violence. But we can all be disruptors. Working with survivors and perpetrators, I've learned a great deal, even as a survivor myself. My work has led me inside detention centers, providing workshops on intimate partner violence and healthy relationships. As the founder of the Eva Lee Parker Foundation, I often receive calls, emails, and messages from family members and friends in desperate need of guidance on supporting and understanding what those they care about are experiencing. As a speaker and workplace trainer, my company, Courageous SHIFT, is often called in to organizations after an incident has occurred. And each day, I read articles or see interviews from neighbors after someone has lost their life due to domestic violence. Unfortunately, I can't answer every call or email, train every manager, develop policies for every organization, or be in every neighborhood. "You Can't Save Us" is my attempt at supporting those who want to be more than just bystanders. They want to be disruptors.

As I mentioned earlier, disruption involves three components: awareness (A), belonging (B), and change (C). In the case of disruption, **Awareness** is knowing about domestic violence, its impact, and the challenges and obstacles facing survivors. **Belonging** involves creating a space for survivors, whether that's them feeling safe to disclose or unlearning harmful beliefs you hold about domestic violence. In **Change**, we delve deeper and examine beliefs, policies, programs, legislation, and our responses to domestic violence. Collectively, they can disrupt domestic violence and, in turn, get survivors the support they need.

Stop Being a Hero

This book is about survivors and how those around them (family, friends, neighbors, employers) can support them in ways that are empowering. As noted in *No One's Coming to Save You*, I don't recommend you be a survivor's savior; actually, you can't. Attempting to do so replicates the same power and control dynamics they have experienced with their partner currently or previously. However, you can be a supporter, and in *You Can't Save Us*, I'll show you how.

Chapter One

Family

"**W**OMEN AGES 18 TO 24 and 25 to 34 generally experience the highest rates of intimate partner violence."[1]

Your family member is in trouble! A number of the messages I receive are often from loved ones of those experiencing intimate partner violence. They share their frustrations, sadness, and anger about the situation. I've been on both sides of these circumstances. As a child, I could not understand why some family members were "accepting" the abuse. As a victim, I know what it's like to have a family member question why I was still in the relationship, even though the person had emotionally and physically harmed me. Whatever the scenario, the reality is that those family members are scared for their loved ones and don't want to lose them to domestic violence.

During a lunch meeting, I was discussing my work with someone. The person shared with me that they have a sister who is in an abusive marriage. They told me about incidents that have occurred over the years and what was the final straw for them. For the most part, they have had no contact with their sister due to their husband. They also shared that their dad still keeps in contact with their sister and her husband, which they found frustrating. I shared that their dad has decided that it's better to remain in the sister's life than to risk not being there when the sister needs him. "It is safer for her to have someone she can turn to. Your dad has chosen to be that person. He seems to know the risk of isolation from family." It was an a-ha moment for the person I was meeting with during our conversation.

To give you a better understanding of what your loved one is going through, here is a list of the different types of victim experiences:

- Pinching, slapping, punching, kicking, and

strangling.

- Name-calling, yelling, threats, insults, and gaslighting.

- Manipulation, blaming them for the abuse, and coercion.

- Isolation, ridicule, and control.

- Being unable to work or being forced to work.

- They are unable to spend money or are forced to give money to their partner.

- Threatening to take the children, kill themselves, or kill a family member or pet.

- Uses religion to keep them obedient.

- Forces them into strict gender roles.

- Inability to disagree or challenge their partner.

Family Dynamics

When a relative is experiencing relationship abuse, it impacts all of their relationships, including with their families. The more power and control the person has over your loved one, the more likely the family dynamics will change. Here are just some of the ways domestic violence impacts family dynamics:

- Missed holidays or special events.

- Shorter visits or no visits at all.

- The family is to blame for the poor relationship.

- Children are kept away from the victim's family.

- The victim no longer participates in family traditions.

- The victim no longer trusts their family.

- Children withdraw from others.

- The victim may become aggressive towards other family members.

- The perpetrator is violent towards other family members, including their own.

- The children are used as weapons against others.

- Your family member feels alone.

Kristie Puckett, Survivor

My family was as supportive as they could be during my abusive relationship. I was a young new mom, and they did their best to support my parenting, my adulthood, and my decisions. When they found out I was being abused, they provided readily available resources to me. I could come home, borrow money when he stole it, and they would co-sign when I needed a new car after he totaled mine. However, they also didn't know how to navigate violence because it wasn't something they had ever experienced.

My child was with me in the house during the abusive relationship, so my family often came to pick him up to remove him from the violence and protect him from exposure. My abuser was not abusive toward my child; in fact, he was very gentle with him. He did witness the vitriol that my abuser directed toward me, and one day, while we were arguing, my

3-year-old told me, "Mama, just be quiet so that he doesn't be mean to you and fight you..." That made me sad. My baby knew I was being mistreated, and that was the day I started figuring out how to get out.

A specific incident I remember is when my brothers were fighting my abuser, and I was more worried about what this meant for them and their careers if the neighbors or anyone else called the police or if they seriously injured him. I also felt incredibly embarrassed that they had to come to my rescue this way. My oldest brother is now a retired firefighter, but when he was working, I lived in his service area for a time and knew some of his coworkers. During a terrible fight, the neighbors called 911 and asked for police, fire, and medical help, and when the firefighters saw me, they recognized who I was. I felt so ashamed that they had to see me that way, and the officer told them, "We come out here all the time and she just won't leave him." I felt so small in that moment and wanted to disappear.

I recognize how hard all of this can be for you. You see your loved one in pain, and you want to fix it. But, you can't fix something that they may not be ready to recognize as broken or desire to be fixed. Additionally, sometimes, as family members, our own experiences with relationship abuse influence how we respond.

Family History of Abuse

Seeing a loved one harmed can bring about all types of emotions, including fear, frustration, and dread. Their experience can also trigger hurtful memories. If you grew up in a household where abuse took place, you may have a hard time understanding why a loved one is in the situation they're in. That's just it. Let's say you and your sister witnessed your mom being abused by your father. It will change you. Now you may have grown up to learn how unhealthy that experience was; however, that may not be the case for your sister. She may have internalized the role of a victim. She may have subconsciously decided that abuse was normal and that she deserved it.

A recurring theme I hear from survivors is that many of them saw domestic violence while growing up. I hear the same from the men I've worked with in the jails. When I ask the female and male inmates if they have ever witnessed a healthy relationship, very few of them say yes. For those who say yes, they also recognize that, as children, they don't know everything that goes on in the adult relationships around them.

It may be hard to come to terms with the fact that history is repeating itself with a family member. While I never wanted to experience relationship abuse, after distance from my own experience, I am not surprised that I did. History will repeat itself if we do not learn from and implement new interventions and tools. If you have a family member experiencing intimate partner violence, it may come a time when you have to reckon with your family's history.

If you were also a victim of relationship abuse, your feelings can go from empathy to anger. You may say to yourself, "Why are they dealing with this? Don't they remember what I went through?" Most likely, they do, but that doesn't change the fact that they are currently experiencing one of the most challenging times of their lives, and judgment won't help.

Adult Children of Survivors

It's essential to recognize that children are severely impacted by witnessing and experiencing domestic violence. We must remember that those children become adults. Suppose interventions, such as individual and family therapy, take place while they are children. In that case, there is a likely chance that the therapist can salvage a relationship between the survivor, the abusive person, and their children. Unfortunately, more often than not, very few children receive the support they need as victims of domestic violence. Those children become adults, and the dynamics between parents/caregivers and them don't always play out well.

While I talk about the empathy family members should give survivors, survivors must recognize the actual impact of what their children experienced and how it has shaped every aspect of their lives. As an adult who witnessed a lot of intimate partner violence growing up, I did not truly understand how it changed me until I was in my thirties and experiencing abuse myself. After finally leaving, one of my main priorities was getting support for my son. There were times when any form of discomfort would send him into an angry spiral. He has every right to be angry, but my goal was to teach him new coping skills and how to regulate his emotions in an age-appropriate way. I didn't always get it right, but therapy for both of us did help tremendously. I didn't want him to grow up and replicate what he had witnessed, whether as a victim or a perpetrator. I did a lot of listening, and there were times he didn't have nice things to say about me. I had to accept that and take ownership of the times I hurt him because of the trauma I was dealing with. Adult children of survivors need grace and patience, too. They experienced something that they could not process or fully understand.

Enovia Bedford, Adult Child of a Survivor

For a long time, I did not see myself as a victim of domestic violence because I wasn't the one being physically hurt. I don't think anyone in my family, including my sibling, looked at us as victims, even though we definitely felt like victims. The pain was constantly around me, like a thick presence in our home, and it made us live in a state of perpetual fear. I remember leaving in the middle of the night to go to Virginia to stay with my mother's best friend and knowing that there were weapons hidden in the house so my mother could feel safe if my father became violent and abrupt in an argument happened. There was no telling what would trigger an argument or how he would respond in certain situations, or how my mother, who was volatile as well, would respond.

There was a time during my pre-teen years when my mother moved to my grandmother's house a block away and left me with my dad. While he was trying to hold his composure, I could see that he was spiraling week after week. I didn't know what was happening at the time, but looking back, I realize he was losing it. He tried to stay in control, but it all boiled over on the day he shot my mother with a shotgun on my grandmother's birthday. I was headed to school, but my mother pulled up and told me to get in the car and said my father had shot her. The police were there, but they didn't realize initially that she had been shot. I started screaming because there was blood everywhere and it was just a gruesome scene to witness that young.

While he was on the run, he would drive by our house. It took months for my dad to be arrested. During that time, he would call, and my family would give me the phone to speak with him. I didn't want to talk to him; however, I felt obligated to by the adults around me. Those were pivotal years of my adolescent life and I was missing days and weeks of school. I also had to learn how to take care of my mother's wound, which no 12-year-old should do. As a mom now, there are things I would not have done or would have done differently.

My relationship with my dad was loving at the time. He was the dad who would pick all the kids up and take them to the amusement park, hang out in the garage, take apart radios and put them back together, and get on the boat and go fishing. At one point, as an adult, I asked him if he planned to shoot my mother and kill himself, what did he think would happen to me. He said he knew my grandmother would do a great job of raising me. He doesn't get it, has zero accountability for the profound harm that he caused, and I've had to block him and go no contact.

As an adult, seeing my mother loved well would have made a positive impact on my dating life. It would've taught me what a truly reciprocal and safe partnership looks like, what it feels like, and how to set up firm boundaries. The pain that I felt when the first man I loved and trusted abandoned me connects back to that foundational pain and the fear of being an afterthought, less than, the abandonment, and not being chosen. I've had to go to therapy for a long time to work through that.

I do wish there had been some kind of family therapy just to help us all cope. It was very traumatic.

When to Set Boundaries

Sadly, there may come a time when you have to set boundaries with your loved one who is experiencing domestic violence. Boundaries are for you. They serve as a reminder of your limitations and how you expect and deserve to be treated. Boundaries do not mean you are giving up on your loved one. You may want to set boundaries if:

- You are in danger or fearful.

- When you have been assaulted or harmed by a loved one's partner.

- When children are involved.

- When the victim becomes aggressive towards you.

- When drugs or alcohol are involved.

Setting healthy boundaries is beneficial to maintaining a relationship with your loved one. Ask yourself what boundaries you need to establish to maintain a healthy relationship with your loved one. Healthy boundaries can look like:

- Not allowing the use of drugs and alcohol in your home when your family member and their partner are around.

- Not allowing aggressive or violent behavior.

- Providing emotional but not financial support.

- Listening without giving advice.

- Having holiday dinners at your place or only going to theirs, so you can control how long you stay.

If your loved one is no longer in the abusive relationship, there is a chance they are still experiencing the impact and long-term effects of it. Give them the space to process what they went through. As a survivor, I know some days are better than others. And, if you really want to support them, give them my book, *No One's Coming to Save You,* to help them navigate life after abuse.

None of this is easy. You may choose to ignore what is happening to them, or you may want to come and save them. The reality is that you can't save them. However, you can support them, but you must recognize your own boundaries, biases, and influences. Let's take a look at how my framework of **Disruption** can be helpful when a family member is experiencing or has experienced domestic violence.

Awareness

6 ways to build awareness as a family member

1. Learn about domestic violence and its impact on the victim.

2. Research your local resources.

3. Consider the challenges, obstacles, and barriers your family member is experiencing that may hinder their ability to leave the relationship. For instance, specific laws and rights of parents or married couples may influence the choices they make.

4. Be aware of your biases and boundaries.

5. Determine what cultural norms you hold that may hinder your support or awareness.

6. Learn about the ways your family members keep themselves safe.

Questions to consider to build your awareness

What do I know about relationship abuse?

What do I know about what the family member is experiencing?

Am I aware of any resources available?

How have current family dynamics impacted my relationship with this person?

What are the challenges, obstacles, and barriers this family member is experiencing that may hinder their ability to leave the relationship?

What are my boundaries?

Am I bringing my own baggage to this situation?

Am I knowledgeable enough about what the family member is experiencing after surviving the abusive relationship?

How are cultural norms impacting me?

Belonging

8 ways to create belonging

1. Create an environment where the family member feels safe to share with you, for instance, by simply calling to check on them and letting them guide the conversation without asking about what is going on.

2. When a situation arises, respond from a place of love and nonjudgment.

3. Ask them how you can support.

4. Have a conversation about what you are willing to do or what you are comfortable with.

5. Whenever possible, disengage or limit your interactions with the abusive person.

6. Invite them over for family game night.

7. Ask them to take a walk in the park with you.

8. Visit them and cook their favorite meal.

Questions to consider to create belonging

Have I created an environment where this family member feels safe to share with me?

How have I responded to situations that have arisen, and could I have responded from a more supportive space?

Have I asked them what they need support with?

Change

8 ways to embrace change

1. Accept that your family member is not ready to leave.

2. Co-create a safety plan with your loved one.

3. Change the way you talk about your loved one from a victim to empowering language.

4. Don't give advice. Just listen.

5. Keep abreast of current legislation that may affect your family member.

6. Volunteer or provide support for your local domestic violence organizations.

7. Learn ways to advocate for your family member.

8. Call out other family members who are judgmental or critical of the survivor.

Questions to consider when creating change

What beliefs do I hold that I need to release?

What new information can I research to provide more context and support?

Can I advocate for the family member?

How can I change the way I show up for this family member?

As hard as it may be to witness, your loved one, with support, can overcome this. While they will be forever changed, that does not mean you all can't rebuild your relationship. You must be willing to accept this new version of themselves, especially if they have been doing the work to heal. It's going to be different, but different doesn't have to be a bad thing. However, it is your responsibility to ensure you are also prepared to be a supportive family member of someone who has experienced intimate partner violence. Continue to ensure you've built your awareness, created a space of belonging, and embrace the changes that are possible.

Your Questions Answered

"Why didn't they tell me sooner?"

There are several reasons why someone experiencing intimate partner violence doesn't share: shame, judgment, ridicule, fear, or they aren't quite sure if they are in an abusive relationship.

"Why don't they just leave?"

Often, leaving isn't just a quick and easy decision. There are many barriers to leaving, including money, housing, safety, isolation, fear, threats, and outright violence. Something to consider is that the deadliest time for a victim is after she leaves an abusive relationship.

"Is it really that serious?"

Yes, it is. Abuse is serious even if the person is never physically assaulted. It is serious (and dangerous) to have your life controlled by someone else.

"What can I do to help without making it worse?"

The most important thing you can do is to educate yourself. By reading this book, you are taking the first step to understanding what your loved one is experiencing. Support for someone experiencing intimate partner violence can range, but should be led by the person being abused.

"Should I confront their partner?"

I would not recommend confronting a partner unless it is absolutely necessary. It can be dangerous not just for you but for the person experiencing the abuse.

"What do I say to the kids?"

What you say to the kids will depend on their age. You have to find an age-appropriate way to bring up the topic. Another approach is to model a healthy relationship, including how to resolve conflicts without resorting to violence.

"How do I support them if they go back?"

If possible, ask them.

You: I understand that you have decided to return to your partner. I want to make sure you are safe and be there for you. Is there a way I can still support you even if it's just listening?

"Why do they defend or protect their abuser?"

Someone who is experiencing abuse will defend or protect the abuser because they have been trained and manipulated into doing so by this person. The abusive person wants them to believe that they are the only people the victim can trust and rely on. Sometimes they defend the abuser because they have normalized the abuse.

"Am I doing enough?"

You can only do what you have the capacity to do <u>and</u> what your loved one is willing to let you do. You are doing enough.

"What resources should I share with them?"

There are national and local resources, as well as cultural and gender-specific resources, available. Try your local domestic violence agency first and branch out from there.

Chapter Two

Friends

"**S**URVIVORS ARE 3 TIMES as likely to meet the criteria for PTSD."[1]

Next to family, friends are a lifeline for someone experiencing domestic violence. However, as friends, we often tend to either cast judgment or seek a way to save them. You may have noticed the red flags before your friend or even shared your concerns, but the friend dismissed them. It can be hard to see your friend go through something so devastating and know that it could have been avoided.

One of the biggest challenges I had during my experience was that most of my closest friends did not live in the same city as I did. So while I was already being isolated, there was the extra loneliness of not having anyone near me. I had a few friends, but most of them I had only just met before getting into the relationship, so we hadn't yet built a solid friendship. Friendships are nurtured over time, and I didn't have that. I leaned on my long-distance friends as much as I could. I would tell them what was going on, but they didn't truly understand what was happening.

However, one of my best friends shared with me after I was out of the abusive relationship that she was very concerned and even called a hotline to get guidance. I shared what she told me in No One's Coming to Save You, and I'll share it here as well. She said, "I called and told them about how he had physically hurt you and that I thought it was going to be over, but you were back with him. I remember the call vividly because I know this sounds judgey, but I was just so confused and shocked about how this could happen to you. You've always been the one not to take any mess. So I couldn't understand why you went back. The hotline helped me understand the dynamics of domestic violence and told me how to support you. I cried the entire time on the phone, but I hung up knowing how to be there for you and give out resources if you ask for them." A good friend will seek out the answers to provide better support.

How it impacts friendships

When a friend is in an abusive relationship, it can and often will take a toll on the friendship. Your friend is being conditioned not to trust you and to separate themselves from you. You may notice that your friend:

- Doesn't hang out as much

- Wears different clothes

- Frequently on the phone during hangouts

- Leaves early or cancels at the last minute

- They bring their partner along without telling you

- Starts to challenge your loyalty

- Drinking more heavily

- Abuses drugs

- Has odd outbursts

- Just seems different

While recognizing these changes is helpful, be mindful of how you approach the subject with your friend. As this person's friend, your intent may be to be supportive, but saying and doing the wrong things can ruin the friendship. You won't always get it right, and you must acknowledge when you may have made a mistake. Avoid these common mistakes:

Minimizing: "It's not like he hit you." Domestic violence involves more than just physical abuse.

Pressuring: "Just leave already." There are many barriers to escaping, including financial, religious, and threats, as well as fear.

Moralizing: "I'd never let a man treat me that way." At one point, every survivor has said that, and that also doesn't mean you have the moral ground because you wouldn't.

Centering themselves: "This is so hard for me to hear." It's not about you. Process your feelings with someone else, but not the survivor.

Peacemaking: "Maybe he's just stressed." That invalidates the survivors' experience, and stress is still no reason to be abusive.

Abandoning: "I didn't know what to say, so I said nothing." Sometimes, saying nothing can do more damage to a friendship than saying the wrong thing. No one wants to feel abandoned.

Don't be surprised if they become defensive. Additionally, your friend may not realize they are in an abusive relationship. Someone can never lay a hand on you and still be abusive and controlling. Your friend may be experiencing some of the following from their partner:

- Manipulation and coercion

- Put others against the friend

- Excessive affection followed by withdrawal

- Silent treatment when they've done something "wrong"

- Told you you aren't a good friend

- Having their reality questioned

- Having their abuse minimized or outright denied

- The partner consistently moves the goalposts

- Partner has vague boundaries

- Claim ignorance

- Changes the criteria of the relationship

"But they are out of the relationship."

Just because your friend is out of the abusive relationship does not mean things will go back to normal. They have experienced a very traumatic time in their life, and it has mentally, emotionally, financially, and even somatically changed them. If you've ever experienced the end of a relationship, you can recall how heartbreaking that can be. Now factor in the abuse they've experienced and imagine what it may be like if they have to coparent with this person, or are fighting addiction, or don't have any place to go. In my book, No One's Coming to Save You, I share the many obstacles survivors face and why focusing on specific areas is vital to navigating their lives after abuse. While friendship is one of them, I encourage you to meet them halfway, maybe even more than halfway. Kindness and grace can go a long way.

Kristie Puckett, Survivor

I needed friends who would listen without judgment. I was already very ashamed of my abuse. I was constantly trying to figure out how I could escape or if I even could, because as the abuse worsened, so did my dependence on and use of cocaine, eventually leading to crack cocaine. Once I started using crack, most of my old friends were replaced by new "friends," but they also had an addiction. I needed friends who could provide a safe place for me to fall when I needed it. I knew better than anyone that I needed to leave, but I also knew I couldn't quite put into words how dangerous it would be for me and them if he thought I was with them and they were protecting or hiding me in some way.

After I left, I needed people to remember that I was still fragile and needed more grace and compassion, even though the immediate danger might have been over. This person was someone I loved deeply, and even though he hurt me repeatedly, it didn't stop my heart from feeling what it felt. Compassion and empathy have to be extended to us as survivors. Can you imagine breaking up with someone you love? And on top of that, they didn't treat you right. My friends were supportive, but some also brought up situations that kept me awake at night, and I was still trying to forget some of the things they mentioned. I was too early in my healing to hear them; timing really is everything.

There is nothing wrong with you wanting to help your friend. You just have to be mindful of your approach and your own experiences. Let's use the ABCs of Disruption framework.

Awareness

5 ways to build your awareness as a friend

1. Recognize how your experience with relationship abuse may influence your thoughts, opinions, and support.

2. Determine the type of abuses your friend may be experiencing. That will guide you on how to show up for them.

3. Consider what you may need to learn more about. For example, you can research how to create a safety plan with a friend or learn about your local laws.

4. Don't take it personally. Your friend is

emotionally overwhelmed by the abuse.

5. Take note of and enforce your boundaries, while also respecting theirs.

Questions to consider to build your awareness

Have you experienced relationship abuse? If so, how might that influence your support?

Are you aware of the various types of abuse your friend may be experiencing?

What topic involving relationship abuse might you need to learn more about?

Belonging

7 ways to create belonging:

1. Create an environment where your friend can turn to you without judgment.

2. You can practice empathy without being critical of your friend's decisions.

3. Invite them to gatherings even if they say no. That shows you still care.

4. Refrain from speaking negatively about their partner, but instead point out inconsistencies when the conversation permits.

5. Allow them to just be. It's not necessary to bring up the situation every time they are around. As a survivor told me, "Create meaningful moments despite the storm."

6. Ask what they need and not what you think they need.

7. Admit when you've made a mistake and be open to rectifying the situation.

Questions to consider to create belonging

Have you created an environment where your friend can turn to you without judgment? Think about the last time you all talked about their partner. Were you critical of the person? Did you point out red flags, but not in a concerned or loving way?

Have you respected their boundaries and not discussed the previous relationship?

Change

5 ways to embrace change:

1. Determine a better approach to the subject with your friend. Review the "Trust-Building Questions" chapter of the book.

2. Let go of beliefs that are unsupportive of your friend.

3. Change the way you engage with the abusive person. You can limit contact or completely disengage.

4. Assist with safety planning if desired or requested.

5. Advocate for legislation that positively impacts the lives of friends like yours.

Questions to consider when embracing change

What's a better way to approach this subject with your friend?

What beliefs do you need to release to be a more supportive friend?

Once you've gone through the framework, you're now ready to support a survivor, whether they are currently in the relationship or free from it.

When to end the friendship

However, there may come a time when it becomes clear that the friendship must come to an end. Sometimes the weight of the abusive relationship is too much for you, or it has become unsafe to maintain the friendship. You'll have a lot of feelings around ending the friendship, and that's okay. You may consider ending the friendship if:

- Your life is in danger

- Your friend has become abusive towards you

- You don't have the capacity to support your friend. It may not be the end of the friendship, but instead a pause. Of course, you don't want anything to happen to your friend, and you can't ignore your capacity to be supportive.

Friendships are beautiful because they are the ones we choose to develop and nurture. Take the time, but still hold space in your heart for reconciliation. Being a friend to someone who is or has experienced relationship abuse can be hard. The friend is going through a life-altering experience, and sometimes they simply cannot or won't be the same person they were previously. Allow flexibility in your friendships. If you desire to maintain the friendship (and I hope you do), be sure to ask them how you can show up as a supportive friend for them. And if the friendship has to take a pause or end, it is still possible to do so with compassion, empathy, and love.

Your Questions Answered

"How do I bring it up without pushing them away?"

Sometimes being direct won't work, and the friend may become defensive. Instead, wait for them to bring up a situation and take it from there. For example:

Friend: Last night we got into an argument because I didn't cook their dinner right. It was so annoying.

You: Yea, that is. I remember you mentioned something similar before. Does that happen often, and how does that make you feel? You are doing your best and deserve to be treated with respect by your partner.

Now, you may not be outright asking, but you are sowing a seed. Let it linger. Let your friend guide the conversation, but it's okay to ask questions that spark their curiosity.

"What if I'm wrong?"

Then you're wrong, and that's okay. In my experience, if someone is concerned that a friend is experiencing relationship abuse, they are hardly ever wrong.

"How can I be supportive without taking sides?"

The better question is, why would you not take the side of the person being harmed? Being supportive also means that you advocate for the friend who is being abused. You can, if possible, hold the abusive person accountable. Take the side of freedom from abuse and harm.

"Why do they keep making excuses for the abuse?"

Your friend has been trained to excuse their experiences. The abusive partner has told them the abuse is their fault, and they've internalized that. Manipulation is a prominent tactic used by people who abuse.

"How do I keep them safe if they won't leave?"

I love this question because there are so many ways to keep someone safe who is still in an abusive relationship. Safety isn't just physical. You can:

- Keep the money they stash away.

- Hold their essential documents.

- Keep a spare set of keys or clothes at your place.

- Being their emergency contact.

- Create a secret phrase that alerts you to take a particular action.

"Should I call the police?"

Depends. Sometimes, calling the police can do more harm than good, while at other times it can be a lifesaver. You need to assess the situation and, if possible, have a conversation with your friend. There may be circumstances in which you should call the police.

"How can I help without burning myself out?"

Burning yourself out supporting a friend who is experiencing domestic violence doesn't benefit anyone. You need to know your capacity to help. Maybe your friend can't stay with you, or you can't talk to them for hours a day after an incident. Determine what you are willing to do and go from there. Remember, the goal isn't to save them, it's to provide them with the support or resources they need to save themselves. It can't, nor should it, fall all on you.

"What if they stop talking to me because I said something?"

That is a real outcome for some friendships. At that point, you will have to love from a distance. You can do random check-ins via call or text. If they don't respond, that's okay. You tried. They have to go through their healing process. However, you may have to accept that the friendship has come to an end.

"Can I report it without their permission?"

You can. Although there may be adverse outcomes, your concerns are valid. I am not telling you whether to report it or not. Only you can assess the situation. I have heard stories of someone reporting abuse, and it saved a friend's life. You decide.

"My friend is out of the relationship but still struggling. What do I do?"

Your friend survived a traumatic experience. You can ask them how you can support them. But as I mentioned in this chapter, your friend has changed. It will take time for them to rediscover themselves. My book, *No One's Coming to Save You*, may be a great tool to help them.

Chapter Three

Neighbors

"**O**VER 25 PERCENT OF women in small rural and isolated areas live more than 40 miles from the closest Intimate Partner Violence Program, compared with less than 1 percent of women living in urban areas."[1]

Do you know your neighbors? What type of conversations are you having with them? What's your "neighbor persona?" A neighbor persona refers to the personality traits you exhibit to the people who live in your community. For example, in your neighborhood, are you known for lugging a bunch of groceries to your place, taking a walk around the block with another neighbor, or standing in front of the building talking about your kids? Oftentimes, our neighbor persona isn't our whole identity, and that's okay. But what happens when the persona of your neighbor doesn't align with what you see or even hear?

During the time I was in the abusive relationship, I lived in an apartment building on the second floor. I had a neighbor who was also a single mom with two sons. She and I would speak and talk a little. She lived directly upstairs from me. One day, after I had been out of the relationship, she and I were talking, and I told her why she hadn't seen the guy around anymore. Afterwards, she said, "I would hear you and him arguing and fighting, but he seems so nice and put together. I wouldn't've thought he would do the things you're describing."

I was taken aback by this comment. What does that even mean? What look was he supposed to have? What look did I give off that makes what he did appear untrue? How are people who abuse supposed to look and behave? Unfortunately, we have many notions of what someone who abuses looks like. They are supposed to look mean, unkempt, aggressive, or out of control. In reality, they can appear quiet, reserved, in control, confident, polished, and friendly, yet still cause us harm.

Domestic violence will look different to everyone, so it's normal not to know what to look for. Some signs of abuse are not as overt as others. Here are a few signs that your neighbor may be experiencing relationship abuse:

- You hear yelling frequently.

- You often see your neighbor crying or screaming.

- Your neighbor cuts your conversations short when their partner is around.

- Your neighbor isn't wearing clothes that are appropriate for the weather.

- Your neighbor doesn't speak to you when their partner is around.

- The partner does all of the talking. `

We live in a society where, as neighbors, we mind our business, and what goes on in another person's home is not our concern. But that's not entirely true and should not be the standard. Building a relationship with your neighbors should be the norm. No, they don't need to know everything, but being in community with them could one day save a life, just as it did for me.

One night, the abuser and I were arguing a lot, much more intensely than other times. I don't know how long it went on, but I just remember thinking, "I need to de-escalate this, I need to leave." I figured that if I left the apartment, then we could be separated and calm down. Unfortunately, when I went to grab the door know, he grabbed me, picked me up, and threw me to the floor. I landed on my ankle and screamed out. I just knew he broke my ankle. He must have known he did something wrong because he opened the door, past my neighbor, and ran outside. My neighbor Stephanie was at my door with a knife in one hand and telling me to come on. I couldn't walk on my ankle. I told my son it was okay for him to come out of his room, and we are safe now. We walked, I wobbled, to her apartment across the hall. It was then that I saw her partner was on the phone with 911. I can never forget that day.

Without Stephanie and her former partner, I don't know if I would be here to tell this story. And, while I did end up forgiving him, I am still so grateful for them stepping in and protecting my kiddo and me. I could never repay them for that act of courage and kindness. Not every neighbor will have to take such drastic measures, but there are ways you can be a supportive neighbor. So, how do you build authentic connections with neighbors so that when you see or hear something, you do something?

Neighbors are often bystanders to abusive relationships. They see and hear most of the fights and arguments. Merriam-Webster defines a bystander as "one who is present but not taking part in a situation or event." Taking it a step further, as a neighbor, you can also be an upstander. An upstander, according to the Oxford Dictionary, is "a person who speaks or acts in support of an individual or cause, particularly someone who intervenes on behalf of a person being attacked or bullied." We have more than enough bystanders and not nearly enough upstanders. Yes, being an upstander takes courage, and it's essential to do so when it's safe and appropriate. There are ways to incorporate being a bystander that can help you transition into becoming an upstander. Being an upstander takes practice, be okay with it not going right the first time. We are not focused on perfection but on effort. List some ways you can become an upstander.

BYSTANDER	UPSTANDER
HEARS AN ARGUMENT ENSUING BETWEEN YOUR NEIGHBORS.	RECORD THE ARGUMENT FOR LATER USE IF NECESSARY.
SEE YOUR NEIGHBOR BEING ASSAULTED.	DISCRETELY TAKE A PHOTO OR VIDEO.
SEE THE BRUISES ON YOUR NEIGHBOR.	ASK IF IT'S OKAY TO TAKE A PHOTO OR VIDEO IN CASE THEY NEED IT LATER.
LISTEN TO THE NEIGHBOR'S STORY OF ABUSE.	ASK WHAT YOU CAN DO TO SUPPORT.
"NOT MY PROBLEM."	RESEARCH LOCAL RESOURCES.
TURN THE TELEVISION UP LOUDER TO DROWN OUT THE NOISE.	DETERMINE IF THE BEST COURSE OF ACTION INVOLVES LAW ENFORCEMENT.

I don't expect everyone to go as far as my neighbors did, but there are steps you can take to be proactive and reactive. Being an upstander does involve taking action; however, only you can determine if it's a risk for your safety. I don't always advise calling law enforcement, but if you can contact them about loud music, you can call them about domestic violence.

Bryan W., Neighbor

One night, my neighbor banged on my door and said her boyfriend had choked [strangled], pushed her down, and kicked her. I knew the guy from my job at a local bar, and he knew me as well. I went over and told him he had to leave, but he refused, so I 'escorted' him out via headlock. He proceeded to beat on her car, so we called the cops. He was arrested, and she stayed at my place for the next two nights out of fear that he would get out and come back. Eventually, she pressed charges, and I went down to the station to give my account of what occurred. He was convicted. They would have verbal arguments, and I would always text her and ask if she was okay. I told her that if she ever needed my help, she to knock on my door or call me. I don't know what happened to him since then, but she and I are still cool.

When not to get involved

Let's be honest, there are times when it's best not to get involved in a domestic violence situation. Here are some situations when you may decide not to engage:

- If the perpetrator is brandishing a weapon, especially a firearm.

- If the perpetrator is threatening you.

- If you determined that the perpetrator is under the influence of drugs or alcohol and has become unreasonable and volatile.

As neighbors, we are often nosy for all the wrong reasons. After reading this chapter, I want you to be nosy for all the right reasons, keeping someone safe. You won't always get it right and I am not asking you to be a hero. However, I do want you to push yourself to understand that domestic violence is impacting your neighborhood, and there are things you can do about it. In homes where abuse is taking place, it can be the smallest acts of kindness that can help a survivor break free. We could all use a good neighbor. Now is your chance to be one.

Here's how you can apply the **Disruption** framework as a neighbor to someone experiencing relationship abuse:

Awareness

10 ways to build awareness as a neighbor

1. Learn about your neighbors.

2. Research the data on domestic violence incidents in your neighborhood.

3. Bring awareness of domestic violence to the attention of your community by talking to your neighbors. Share what you've learned, but not about any specific person or family.

4. Learn about your local domestic violence advocates and agencies, as well as the services they provide.

5. Keep a record of the domestic violence point person at your local police station.

6. Determine the type of relationship you have with your neighbors and identify if it needs improvement.

7. Be aware of any cultural norms, beliefs, and biases you have about domestic violence.

8. Know the warning signs that your neighbor is experiencing abuse.

9. Create a log of what you hear or see.

10. Knock on the door and ask for something. This disruption can be helpful.

Questions to consider to build your awareness

What are your neighbors' names?

   What beliefs or biases do you have about domestic violence?

   What were the outcomes of witnessing domestic violence among your neighbors?

Are you aware of any law enforcement engagement?

What type of relationship would you like to have with your neighbors?

Belonging

10 ways to create belonging

1. Invite your neighbors to dinner or a cookout.

2. Invite their children over to play.

3. Host a game night.

4. Help them with taking in their groceries or fixing something in their home.

5. Talk to them when their partner isn't around or it's safe to do so.

6. Offer to provide basic needs like food or household goods.

7. Be kind. Be present.

8. Be protective of their privacy. There's no need to share their situation with the other neighbors.

9. Offer help.

10. See them as more than just a victim. Speak to them with dignity. Not pity.

Questions to consider to create belonging

How have you been intentional about getting to know your neighbors?

Have you created a relationship built on trust? How will you?

Change

10 ways to embrace change

1. Learn upstander techniques to support your neighbor.

2. Document what you have witnessed.

3. Keep the number of your local domestic violence agency in your phone for easy access.

4. Create a neighborhood program or initiative that addresses and discusses domestic violence.

5. Release any beliefs or biases you hold that hinder how you can support your neighbor.

6. Check your judgmental neighbors.

7. Silence is deadly. Openly talk about domestic violence and how it impacts everyone.

8. Stop normalizing unhealthy and abusive

relationships.

9. Listen to survivors when they tell you what they need.

10. Advocate for the other areas that impact domestic violence (e.g., affordable housing and childcare, legislation, and workforce development). It may not affect you, but it may help others tremendously.

Questions to consider when embracing change

What community policies (HOA rules, etc.) are in conflict with providing support to a neighbor experiencing domestic violence?

How does community policing impact survivor support?

How can you engage grassroots organizations in community building around domestic violence?

You're not a superhero and that's okay. Survivors don't need superheroes; we just need people who care. Even as a neighbor, there are ways you can disrupt domestic violence. It can be small acts of kindness and encouragement, or larger ones, such as keeping a spare set of clothes at home for the survivor. Whether big or small, as survivors, we never forget the people who helped us during our darkest hour. Remember, domestic violence isn't just a problem between two people but something that impacts every neighbor, neighborhood, and community.

Your Questions Answered

"I heard something scary—should I call 911?"

That depends on what you specifically heard. If you hear something loud and sudden or that's getting progressively worse, it's not a bad idea to call 9-1-1.

"What if I make things worse by getting involved?"

Getting involved can vary depending on the circumstances. By asking this question, I surmise that you're really asking, "If I get involved, is it my fault that my neighbor gets hurt?" The answer is no. Abuse is always the fault of the person who is being abused. No one else is causing them to do it (although that is a lie they often tell their victims).

"Is it really my business?"

Domestic violence is everyone's business because it impacts everyone. As a neighbor, if you are repeatedly witnessing your neighbor being abused, you are experiencing vicarious trauma.

"Can I stay anonymous if I report it?"

Yes and no. You can report an incident of abuse to law enforcement and your report will remain anonymous to anyone outside of the legal system. However, law enforcement, 9-1-1, etc., will have a record of your call. However, don't let that stop you from doing what you think is best for the person experiencing the abuse in the moment.

"Should I talk to the person being abused?"

Suppose you've built the type of relationship where you can, go for it. Refer to the "Powerful and Empathetic Questions" chapter for examples of questions you can ask. You can also talk to them about things outside of their relationships. That allows them to create a sense of normalcy in their lives.

"What if the abuser finds out I said something?"

That is a real risk. Do what you need to do to protect yourself, including denying and lying if necessary. You don't owe that person the truth.

"How do I protect my own family while helping?"

Anytime it's between your family and helping, choose your family. If helping puts your family in danger, stop helping. Determine what helping looks like for you. It may not be intervening, but instead calling your neighbor's family if something happens. Sometimes we think we have to do a lot to help someone experiencing relationship abuse, when it can be the little things that are just as meaningful.

"What signs should I be looking for?"

Some signs that your neighbor is in an abusive relationship are that the victim only talks to you when their partner isn't around. You hear loud noises or arguments coming from their place. Check out the resources list in the back of this book for more information.

"Do I need to document what I've seen or heard?"

It's a good idea to keep a record of things you hear or see. While you may never have to share it with anyone, the survivor may need it once they have chosen to leave.

"What community resources can I refer them to?"

The national hotline and your local state coalition are great places to start when you are looking for community resources.

Chapter Four

Employers and Colleagues

"**D**OMESTIC VIOLENCE ISSUES LEAD to nearly 8 million lost days of paid work each year, the equivalent of over 32,000 full-time jobs." [1]

If you are a colleague, supervisor, manager, or part of the leadership team and picked up this book, I want to thank you. It's so easy to dismiss domestic violence as something that isn't your concern. However, the truth is that the impact of relationship abuse goes beyond the four walls of an employee's home. When I was experiencing intimate partner violence (IPV) from 2013 to 2016, I hid it well from my colleagues; rather, I thought I did. At least one of them mentioned thinking something wasn't right. It was in 2015 when domestic violence showed up in my workplace.

Sometime in May of that year, my abuser and I had been arguing for hours. I don't recall what the argument was about, but I remember being taken to the hospital by the medic because I could not walk on my right foot. It turned out that when he picked me up and threw me to the ground, he sprained my ankle. The next day, after getting a temporary restraining order, I had to walk into where I worked on crutches.

To say I was embarrassed is an understatement. At the time, my supervisor and COO responded appropriately and swiftly. That's because they had practice. I was not the first employee who had experienced domestic violence while working there. They took action: printing out a copy of his photos for the front desk and security, giving me a flexible schedule for appointments and safety, and much more. I am sure it was to their chagrin when I said it was okay for him to come to the office again. I went back.

Many survivors repeatedly return to their abusers. The statistics vary, but victims can take up to seven times to leave due to the many obstacles when trying to escape. I left the relationship for the last time in March of 2016, but that was not without its challenges that showed up at my workplace in various ways. I am grateful for my supervisor and COO, who supported me in ways many other survivors didn't get to experience.

After listening to and working with survivors of domestic violence as a speaker and certified professional life coach, I've learned about the impact abuse has on employees and gained insight into how employers can better support and protect them. Some survivors have shared that they lost their jobs, were ostracized, told to make the person stop calling, or pushed to quit. I believe many employers just don't know how to handle the situation or don't clearly understand how domestic violence impacts the workplace.

What I share in this chapter is not an exhaustive list of how intimate partner violence shows up in the workplace. I share examples of how it manifests, what to do, what not to do, and provide resources. I make no guarantees that all of the answers to addressing domestic violence in the workplace are in this chapter. I encourage all employers to train themselves and their staff to take a proactive approach, recognize the signs, and respond to domestic violence incidents. Please speak with your lawyer regarding legal protection and other legal matters.

Domestic violence is by no means the sole responsibility of employers to combat it, but organizations can no longer ignore it. Knowing what an employee is experiencing can guide how you address the situation. I'll say this often: not every person experiences intimate partner violence the same way. Here are a few of the experiences of survivors:

- Their current or former partner is stalking them, including showing up at their workplace and cyberstalking.

- They are being threatened with assault against themselves, children, or pets, removal of their immigration status, contacting you, or "outing" them to family and friends.

- Difficult or expensive custody agreements or court appearances.

- Violation of restraining or protective orders.

- Being forced to work or hand over their money to the abuser.

- Verbal abuse such as name-calling, yelling, criticizing, blaming, and minimizing the abuse.

- Isolation from family, friends, and workplace colleagues.

- Physical abuse such as slapping, kicking, biting, pinching, and punching.

How domestic violence impacts the workplace

While I will list the ways domestic violence impacts the workplace and what the employee may experience at home, I want to provide context. There was a time when companies wanted their employees to focus only on work. They did not want to hear about what was going on in their personal lives. It was a culture of "leave it at the door." In some cases, that was beneficial, such as for surgeons or therapists. However, the reality is that it's impossible to separate the two. Your home life will impact your work life and vice versa. We can't ignore the personal lives of our employees and think that they won't spill over into our professional ones. Here are just some of the ways domestic violence impacts the workplace:

- Decreased productivity. Employees experiencing abuse may not be as productive as they once were before the abuse or as the abuse escalates.

- Increase security and safety risks including workplace violence incidents.

- Loss of focus or emotional distress.

- Decreasing creativity.

- Increase financial implications.

- Decrease employee morale.

- Negative workplace culture.

- Legal liabilities.

- Increased absenteeism.

- Health problems.

- Increased workloads.

- Workplace sabotage.

Recognizing when an employee is in an abusive relationship

Now that you know the impact, how do you recognize the signs that an employee is experiencing relationship abuse? Depending on your interactions with the employee, it may be easier or harder to know. However, it's still important to be aware of the signs just in case. Below is by no means a complete list of signs that an employee is in an abusive relationship, but it is a start. Not every employee will experience domestic violence in the same way.

- Changes in behavior or mood.

- Frequent absenteeism.

- A partner or ex is disrupting their day.

- The partner or ex is showing up unexpectedly at the workplace.

- Employee refuses to have their camera on during virtual meetings.

- The employee is withdrawn or disengaged.

- The employee is consistently unable to work overtime, which was not always the case.

- The employee has come to work with bruises or is wearing clothes that do not match the season.

- The employee appears to be constantly distracted.

- The employee shows signs of exhaustion.

- The employee is missing deadlines.

- The employee is consistently late, leaves early, or stays late.

- The employee will often apologize for even minor things.

- The employee is taking or receiving personal calls more frequently.

- The employee may show signs of aggressive behavior and anger.

- Employees find it challenging to speak with the employee.

- The employee shows symptoms of depression and anxiety.

Lewis Lee, Black Male Survivor

I was in a relationship with someone for two years. Before this incident, there were times when I came to work stressed and still processing arguments we may have had the night before, and I was unsure what I would experience after I got home from work. I would experience anxiety during the day, with my heart beating fast from the text messages I would receive. Normally, I can compartmentalize, but then you start to replay things in your mind, and it starts slowing down my productivity. My production would be cut in half on the days she and I were going through things. Most of the time during the relationship, work was my safe space.

Ultimately, I decided that I no longer wanted to be in the relationship. She tried to reach out to me on different platforms, like social media, and called my phone from other numbers, but I just kept blocking her. One Saturday night, I was at home watching football when I heard a knock on the door. I asked who is it was, and no one answered. I cracked the door open and then she forced her way into my house. Being a man and a Black man at that, I can't just physically remove her in that way; I would've physically removed anyone else. I decided to go outside, get the license plate number, and call the police. She's still in the house, sitting on the couch and saying, 'I'm not leaving until you talk to me.' She didn't realize what I was doing. She comes to the door and sees that I am on the phone with the police. I was in the middle of giving the license plate number, and she immediately came running, kicking, and punching me. I'm trying to hold her off with one hand while still being on the phone, trying to give them the information. I was able to provide them with the information, but she was able to punch me in the face. She then speeds off in the car. My eye was hurting on Sunday, but I was thinking it would go away.

When I woke up on Monday morning, it had blackened and was swollen. I said to myself, "Welp. I still have to go to work." It was a sunny day, so I thought I would be able to get away with wearing sunglasses. But, unfortunately for me, at the time, I worked directly across from my manager. I said hi to everyone, sat down, and started working. An hour goes by and she asks, 'Why do you have those shades on and you're inside?' I said, 'You know it's bright in here.' She replied, 'If you don't take those shades off.' I took the shades off and she said, "What's wrong with your eye?" I didn't say anything. She asked again.

I put my head down and shook my head. She said, "Log out and come to the back. Let's talk." She said 'What's going on? Talk to me." And, I told her everything that happened. She asked if I had told the police. I told her I made a report. She said, "No, go down there and make sure they are going to press charges." She made me clock out and I went to the magistrate to take care of things. She also said that if I needed to take a couple of days, I could.

My manager handled my situation very well. She followed up with me and reminded me that if I needed anything, just ask. She definitely created a safe space for me. Having a supportive supervisor like her, which was a first for me, meant everything. I appreciated that I could even share that in a workspace, and I felt supported.

What to do and not do

Now, you suspect that your employee or colleague is experiencing relationship abuse, and you are aware of the types of abuse and challenges they are facing. You want to be supportive or confirm your suspicions. You may be inclined to ask outright, and in some cases, that may be the best approach. However, I want to provide you with some options to engage with the employee that demonstrate compassion, respect, and privacy. The questions I am providing can be recurring, one-off, or build on each other. Remember, these questions are just a guide, and you should factor in the type of relationship you have with your employee or colleague. Have you all talked about your personal relationships before? Have you shared any private topics with them? Have they been receptive to sharing their personal lives? Refer to Chapter Five for a list of powerful questions you can ask someone who may be experiencing intimate partner violence.

Sometimes what you do or don't do will depend on the circumstances and the employee's experience. Let's take a few of the experiences I mentioned above and determine how to handle them.

Stalking

WHAT TO DO	WHAT NOT TO DO
When informed about stalking, implement safety precautions such as locking doors, banning the accused from the premises, consulting with security about ways to keep employees safe, reevaluating safety protocols, and discussing blind spots with security experts.	Do not expect the victim to control the situation.
Remember that the victim has no control over the stalker.	Do not share the victim's details with other employees.
Offer the victim flexible hours to disrupt established routines.	Don't ignore the problem when a victim discloses.
If necessary, inform your local police department.	Don't give information about the employee to anyone over the phone or without prior consent.
If the perpetrator is an employee of your organization, determine the legal implications of their employment.	
Check if a suspected perpetrator has used company resources to stalk and/or harass the victim.	

Threats

WHAT TO DO	WHAT NOT TO DO
If an employee shares that they have received a threat, take it seriously.	Don't blame the victim.
Consult your security team to ensure safety for victims, employees, clients, and customers.	Don't take it lightly.
Train security to perform threat assessments.	Don't assume the victim can control the threat(s).
Work with security, human resources, employee assistance program staff, managers, and supervisors to create a safety plan for all employees.	Don't force the employee to take leave.
Get as much detailed information about the threat as the victim will provide.	
If the threat is imminent, call 9-1-1.	

Financial Abuse

WHAT TO DO	WHAT NOT TO DO
Pay employees a living wage.	**Don't terminate an employee experiencing domestic violence.**
Close the gender wage gap within your organization.	
Provide resources to food assistance programs.	
Provide resources to financial literacy programs, such as the Allstate Foundation's Moving Ahead Curriculum.	
Offer opportunities for promotions, professional development, mentorship, and sponsorship.	
Speak with an attorney on the legal rights of someone experiencing domestic violence.	
Determine if your employee is eligible for the federal Family and Medical Leave Act (FMLA).	
Determine your state's laws regarding domestic violence in the workplace.	

Emotional and Mental Abuse

WHAT TO DO	WHAT NOT TO DO
Offer health and wellness programs or opportunities at your organization.	Don't try to determine what is or is not emotional and mental abuse.
Display resources and information about emotional and mental abuse.	Don't threaten to terminate or reduce the hours of the employee.
Have someone speak to employees about emotional and mental abuse.	Don't suggest couples therapy.
	Don't ignore the signs.

When an employee is accused of abuse

It can be complicated to determine if an employee is a perpetrator of domestic violence. Perpetrators are skilled at pretending and hiding their abusive behaviors. Many of the survivors I spoke with shared that they were shocked when they told others about the abuse because the person "didn't look like an abuser." There is no look to an abuser. Many organizations have policies on using work time and resources for personal use. If an employee is accused of intimate partner violence, determine if the employee violated any work policies. If no policy is in place, consider drafting and implementing one.

As you investigate accusations that an employee has committed domestic violence, you will want to determine if there are any safety issues for the organization and its employees, speak with an attorneys about employer and employee rights, report concerns to relevant departments, and have a safety plan when asking an employee to leave work premises, turn in work equipment, and if you've decided to terminate their employment. Here are some signs an employee may be a perpetrator of domestic violence:

- Uses abusive language towards colleagues.

- Uses work email to harass partner.

- Blames others for their mistakes.

- Can not take criticism.

- Refuses to acknowledge poor work performance.

- Insist they are always right.

- Consistently leaves work early without

explanation.

- Trembling or shaking.

- Clenched jaws and fists.

- Loud talking or yelling.

- Name-calling coworkers.

- Brief employee work history.

- Demonstrates violence towards people or objects.

- Argumentative.

- Often doesn't cooperate with others.

- Erratic behavior.

- Few family and friends.

- Has an arrest record for domestic violence.

- They appear controlling when around their partner.

- Speaks negatively about their partner or the gender of their partner.

Workplace violence is a serious matter that many organizations should address. Often, organizations recognize the importance of having a plan in place when violence occurs. However, many organizations do not realize the direct correlation between workplace violence and domestic violence. According to the National Institute for Occupational Safety and Health (NIOSH), a personal relationship is one of the four types of workplace violence.[2] Ninety-four percent (94%) of corporate security and safety directors at companies nationwide rank domestic violence as a high-security concern. [3] Employers who fail to protect their employees, including those experiencing domestic violence, from violence at work may be held liable. Don't wait until it's at your door to take action.

The role of workplace policies and training

It would be unrealistic to assume that every human resources leader and COO understands the dynamics of domestic violence and therefore will know how to address its impact on the workplace. However, as you know, employers invest in the protection of their businesses. Addressing domestic violence is doing just that. According to the Centers for Disease Control and Prevention (CDC), "domestic violence issues lead to nearly 8 million lost days of paid work each year, the equivalent of over 32,000 full-time jobs."[4] If you perform a search of "killed at work" and "domestic violence," more than 20,000 news articles would pull up, with many stating a woman was killed at her place of work or a bystander who intervened was murdered. However, there are steps you can take to mitigate the harm.

A 2013 survey by the Society of Human Resources Management (SHRM) found that twenty-one percent of full-time employed adults said they were victims of domestic violence, and seventy-four percent of that group said they've been harassed at work.[5] Something to note: Much of the data around domestic violence and the workplace is at least 20 years old. That doesn't mean the information isn't relevant or should be ignored. What it does tell us is that more research needs to be done. In the meantime, there are two key areas your organization can address domestic violence: training and policy.

Training and Policies

According to a 2023 survey by Training Magazine, large companies' training budgets exceeded $16 million, while mid-sized companies allocated $1.5 million, and smaller companies allocated just under $460,000.[6] Additionally, there is a policy for everything. Many of them are legally mandatory and vary by industry, but there are plenty that are optional. Which of these policies does your organization currently have?

- Equal Employment Opportunity

- Leave and time off

- Remote work

- Grievance

- Drug and alcohol

- Social media

- Confidentiality

- Whistleblower

- Code of conduct

- Anti-harassment and discrimination

- Dress code

- Company property use

- Health and safety

- First aid and emergency procedure

- Disciplinary action

- Data protection and privacy

- Conflict of interest

- Compensation and benefits

- Travel

The same survey by SHRM discovered that sixty-five percent (65%) of companies do not have a formal workplace domestic violence prevention policy.[7] If an organization has a domestic violence workplace policy, it is often included in its anti-harassment and discrimination policies or code of conduct. However, does it truly outline the procedures to follow if an employee discloses abuse or how an employee can seek help?

You may be thinking that even your organization of fewer than 20 people won't be impacted by domestic violence. Let me tell you the story of Humanity Communications Collective (HCC). CEO Yanira Castro founded HCC, a boutique, social justice-driven communications group focused on making real connections. I have known Yanira for nearly a decade, as your children attended the same school. At one point, I even worked for her agency as a communications subcontractor. Yanira was well aware of the work I do, and the first thing she said when she asked if we could chat was, "I didn't think I would ever need your services for my team of 12."

Yanira shared with me that an employee had disclosed to her supervisor that she was experiencing relationship abuse. Yanira jumped into action. After our conversation and my assessing their needs, we decided to go with training for the leadership team, one-on-one coaching for the employee experiencing the abuse, guidance and support for the supervisor, and a comprehensive Domestic Violence Workplace Policy tailored for their specific needs and capabilities. The outcomes: The employee felt supported, was able to ask for and meet her needs, including time off for court dates, excelled in her role, including receiving a promotion, the leadership team felt equipped to support their employees, and now the organization has a blueprint they can refer to if ever needed again. Oh, and they didn't have to replace their employee. By hiring me to provide training, coaching, consulting, and policy development, HCC saved nearly $20,000 in direct and indirect costs associated with replacing her employee. Here are the benefits of providing training and having a Domestic Violence Workplace Policy:

- In the long term, it can save your organization money (including security, employee acquisition, and healthcare costs).

- Employees feel supported and protected.

- It can possibly protect you from legal and liability implications.

- Increased safety for your employees.

- Improved employee retention, loyalty, and morale.

- Compliance with local and federal laws.

- Better risk management.

- Demonstrated corporate social responsibility.

- Your managers and supervisors feel equipped to support their team members.

The beauty of the **Disruption** framework is that employers can apply it to any circumstance, including the workplace. Here's how you can apply the **Disruption** framework as an employer, manager, or colleague to someone experiencing relationship abuse:

Awareness

7 ways to build awareness as an employer

1. Learn about the impact of domestic violence on the workplace.

2. Create opportunities for others to learn.

3. Learn about the experiences of relationship abuse on the employee.

4. Bring in a domestic violence speaker.

5. If you have a domestic violence workplace policy, remind employees about it at least twice a year, as well as during the onboarding

process.

6. Utilize materials such as handouts, handbooks, flyers, posters, and newsletters.

7. Learn about the less obvious signs of domestic violence. Not all abuse is physical.

Questions to consider to build your awareness

What are the gaps in our current employee training that do not address domestic violence?

What books can you read to learn more about domestic violence?

Belonging

9 ways to create belonging

1. Prioritize employee wellness, which includes mental health.

2. Create a culture of acceptance of vulnerability.

3. Make opportunities to build interpersonal relationships between employees.

4. Actively and consistently practice empathy.

5. Ensure your workplace is one of physical and psychological safety.

6. Implement trust-building practices among team members.

7. Create and hold a brave space for a survivor. If someone in your life is or was experiencing abuse, make time to listen.

8. Keep a list of local and national resources in an accessible place.

9. Develop an ERG specifically for domestic violence. The participants can be trained to support an employee who is experiencing relationship abuse.

Questions to consider to create belonging

What do you need to experience a sense of belonging at your organization?

Is the process of sharing challenges welcoming and safe to all employees? If not, what's missing?

Change

9 ways to embrace change

1. Reevaluate your current domestic violence workplace policy.

2. If you don't have one, work with an expert to create your domestic violence workplace policy.

3. Train all employees to recognize the signs of domestic violence and how to respond.

4. Pay a livable wage, as survivors are more often than not experiencing financial and economic abuse.

5. Reconsider your thoughts on victims and perpetrators. They don't have a specific "look" or are of a particular socioeconomic level.

6. Volunteer at your local domestic violence shelter, hotline, or grassroots organization.

7. Be aware of the domestic violence workplace laws in your state.

8. Incorporate your domestic violence workplace policy into your workplace violence policy.

9. During a crisis, reach out to a professional for guidance.

Questions to consider when embracing change

What are the barriers to developing a survivor-centered domestic violence workplace policy?

How can your organization incorporate domestic violence awareness in their corporate social responsibility goals?

It can appear to be daunting to address the issue of domestic violence in the workplace. When determining if you'll do so, consider how much the benefits outweigh the work. By developing ways to address domestic violence, you are reducing the financial burden it places on your organization, decreasing safety and security risks, and, most importantly (in my opinion), showing your employees that you care and value their employee wellness.

Your Questions Answered

"What is my legal responsibility if I know an employee is experiencing domestic violence?"

There are different state and federal laws. Be sure to speak with an attorney for legal advice.

"How do I support the employee without overstepping or making things worse?"

The best way to avoid overstepping is to recognize when you should take a step back. That could be a change in the person's demeanor or conversation, or you may be asked to stop asking. You can always periodically ask the employee how they are doing or remind them that you are available to support them.

"Should I involve HR, legal, or security—and when?"

There may not be a right time to involve them. Still, the best approach would be to see that the situation with the employee is escalating or an imminent threat is taking place, which would be the time to involve HR, legal, or security. HR could also be involved if the employee is requesting time off outside of standard practice, needs replacement work equipment, or asks for a new work email address. You should include security when the abusive person is on the premises.

"How can we protect the employee and the rest of the staff if there's a safety risk?"

The first step would be to inform security, especially if the risk is imminent. That may also be the best time to call law enforcement. If you have an active shooter protocol, that can also come in handy. If you don't have any protocols, reach out to a threat assessment professional who understands explicitly the dynamics of intimate partner violence.

"What if the employee doesn't want help?"

If the employee doesn't want help, there's nothing you can do about it. However, quarterly reminders of the resources available to all employees can be beneficial.

"Can I fire or discipline someone if their personal situation is affecting their work performance?"

Legally, you will need to determine if firing them falls under any state or federal laws. Ethically, you can take a different approach. While you must maintain workflow, remember this person doesn't want to be in this situation, but may have many barriers or obstacles to escaping. Have a conversation with them about their work performance and ask what they need to get back on track. It may take some flexibility and empathy, but it's possible to retain an employee who is experiencing domestic violence. Additionally, discuss your concerns with your HR lead or an HR consultant if you have access to one. There is nothing wrong with holding an employee accountable, just be sure you have all of the information and details to do so empathetically.

"What accommodations can or should we provide?"

Accommodations will vary depending on the employee's circumstances. Some accommodations that they may need include flexible work schedules, changing office locations, new email addresses, or removal of their names from websites and social media. Discuss with the employee what accommodations may be helpful and negotiate from there.

"How do we train managers and staff to recognize and respond appropriately?"

Hire a professional. Seriously, the best training will be from someone who not only knows the information and data but also has lived experience.

"What community or national resources should we refer employees to?"

There is always the National Domestic Violence Hotline. You can also search for "domestic violence help" and "[your city/town/state]" to find resources in your area. Additionally, if you are in the United States, every state has a domestic violence coalition. Coalitions are a great resource to find more community-based and local organizations.

"How do I talk to an employee I suspect is experiencing abuse without offending or scaring them?"

Stick to what you've observed, rather than what you think may be happening. Focus on the facts. Chapter Five provides a list of questions you can ask someone you think may be experiencing relationship abuse.

"How do I create a workplace culture where people feel safe disclosing abuse?"

By talking about it, often and openly, and reminding all employees of the resources available. If you have a culture where all employees can bring their whole selves, you are building a culture of support. Within your Domestic Violence Workplace Policy, you want to have a protocol for employees to feel safe to disclose abuse.

"What kind of messaging should we use to show that our company takes domestic violence seriously?"

Your messaging includes details about confidentiality and support, ensuring that employees do not have to worry about retaliation or job loss. Part of my services includes developing your organization's specific internal communications plan. However, you can also collaborate with your communications team to develop the appropriate language and messaging.

Chapter Five

Trust-Building Questions for Survivor-Centered Support

T HESE QUESTIONS ARE NOT intended to be the sole way you have a conversation with someone experiencing relationship abuse. They are a guide. Take your time and lead with compassion, curiosity, and empathy.

General Well-Being or Surface-Level Check-ins

These questions are low-pressure and allow for rapport-building.

1. How are you feeling today?

2. You're not quite yourself today; want to talk about it?

3. What worries you most?

4. Are you experiencing any anxiety as it relates to home?

5. Is there anything occurring at home that is distracting you from work?

6. How can I show up for you as a friend?

7. How can I best support you?

8. When you are experiencing challenges, how can I best support you?

9. What do you need, and how can we help you?

10. What support do you need from me as your manager/supervisor?

Begins to Explore Needs or Home Life

These require some trust and willingness to share but aren't explicitly triggering.

1. How are things going at home?

2. If you could change one thing in your life right now, what would it be?

3. What resources do you think you may need to support you?

4. Would you be okay with me checking in periodically to ensure you are safe?

5. Is there anything you'd like me to know about your relationship that you're hesitant to share?

Implied Relationship Issues or Abuse Indicators

These may raise red flags and are appropriate with more trust or clear context.

1. Does your partner make you not feel good about yourself?

2. How does your partner treat you at home?

3. How is your children's relationship with your partner?

4. Do you feel safe in your relationship?

5. Are you safe at home or in your relationship?

Safety/Readiness/Barriers to Action

These require vulnerability, introspection, and may activate trauma or concern.

1. Are you safe?

2. Are you in immediate danger?

3. Are you afraid of your partner? Do you feel you are

in danger?

4. What would happen if you did make a change to your current situation?

5. What would happen if you didn't make a change to your current situation?

6. Knowing yourself and your circumstances, what obstacles might get in the way of you taking action?

7. If you are ever in trouble or danger, is there anyone you would like me to contact on your behalf?

Remember: Never ask "why don't you just leave?" We want to empower survivors!

Chapter Six

Conclusion

F IRST, I WANT TO thank you. Seriously. It took a lot of courage to pick this book up (or download it) and decide it's something worth reading. Not because you don't care, but more so because domestic violence is a complex and scary topic. We see the stories online about just how dangerous intimate partner violence is, and it can drive you to disengage. However, as I said in the introduction, relationship abuse impacts every aspect of our lives.

As Kristie shared in her story of her family picking up her son, sometimes it's the smallest acts that are helpful ot the survivor. Enovia's story of being a child and experiencing her mother being harmed and her father not taking accountability left a lasting impact on her life. As a loved one, what if you took the extra step to support your family member and their children? Imagine the profound and positive impact that would have.

Being a friend to someone who is or has experienced relationship abuse can be overwhelming. Consider, during your darkest time, what you needed from your friends. Grace? Empathy? Loyalty? You know your friend deserves better, and eventually, they will realize it too. But for now, be the friend that listens without judgment, finds out information about local resources like my best friend did, or takes their mind off of things with a fun night out.

From personal experience, I know neighbors can be vital to a survivor's safety and even just supporters. Again, you don't have to go as extreme as shared in that chapter, but your acts of kindness can be the disruption needed to help survivors. Find out ways you can move from bystander to upstander. Having a neighbor as an upstander can give a survivor the tools and courage to break free. Plus, it makes for a caring, thriving, and violence-free community, and who doesn't want that?

Employers, I get it, you may think that domestic violence isn't your concern or that you don't have the tools to address it. Remember the simple act of asking what's wrong that Lewis' supervisor did to support him and make a difference in his life. If, after reading the "Employer" chapter, you still don't think it's your problem, contact me. Please. I need to know where I missed connecting the dots. From the impact on financials, safety, productivity, and employee wellness, organizations must take domestic violence seriously.

Ultimately, for the disruption of domestic violence to take place, you must build your awareness, create a space for belonging, and embrace change. You are not required or even asked to be the hero; survivors will save themselves. But, disruption is a beautiful thing. And, all it takes is your ABCs; how simple is that! You don't have to perform all of the tools I suggested. Instead, focus on one part of the framework and one action you will take. For example, if your family member is experiencing relationship abuse, you decide you want to create a space of belonging. Ask if you can come over and cook with them. It's the simple act of normalcy that can make a huge difference.

Remember, you are not here to save us. Don't put so much pressure on yourself to fix things. You're not the superhero. You are the family member, friend, neighbor, employer, or colleague who has decided to disrupt domestic violence, and for that, all survivors are grateful!

Acknowledgements

To every corporation, nonprofit, coalition, and business owner who trusted me to share my story, train their employees, and develop their policies.

Lynn Fairweather of Presage Consulting & Training, you took a chance and shared your expertise and experience being a domestic violence speaker and business owner. Thank you for responding to my DM.

Yanira Castro, you have been such a supporter both personally and professionally.

Representative Terry M. Brown, Jr. for seeing the value in my lived experience in developing survivor-centered legislation in North Carolina.

Mia, thank you for always holding me accountable but also reminding me of just how powerful I am and making sure I have a good time.

Kelley, your grounding spirit soothes my soul. Thank you for being one of my biggest cheerleaders.

Tah, your prayers have been literal lifesavers for me. I'm grateful to have you in my life.

My board members. Your support of the Eva Lee Parker Foundation at the ground level has pushed me to new limits.

My family and friends, too many to name, who have held space for me and saw me when I couldn't see myself. This year was one of my most challenging but y'all never let me give up. I am forever grateful.

And as always, to my kiddo. Thank you for every hug and kiss. I love you in every lifetime.

Resources

National Resources

1. Courageous SHIFT. www.CourageousSHIFT.com

2. Gay, Lesbian, Bisexual and Transgender Nat'l Hotline. 888.843.4564. Youth - 800.246.7743. Senior - 888.234.7243. https://lgbthotline.org/

3. Local Domestic Violence Agencies. Many areas have 24-hour hotlines.

4. Love is Respect. 866.331.9474. Text: loveis to 22522. https://www.loveisrespect.org/

5. National Domestic Violence Hotline. 800.799.7233. Text: SMART TO 88788. https://www.thehotline.org/

6. National Indigenous Women's Resource Ctr. 855.649.7299. https://www.niwrc.org/

7. National Sexual Assault Hotline. 800.656.HOPE (4673). https://rainn.org/

8. StrongHearts Native Helpline. 844.762.8483. https://strongheartshelpline.org/

Books

1. Bonomi, Amy et al. *Recantation and Domestic Violence: The Untold Story.* New York: Rutledge, 2024.

2. Cheung, Kylie. *Survivor Injustice: State-sanctioned Abuse, Domestic Violence, and The Fight for Bodily Autonomy.* California: North Atlantic Books, 2023.

3. Coleman, Chrisena. *Just Between Girlfriends: African-American Women Celebrate Friendship.* New York: One World/Ballantine Books, 1998.

4. Gross, Melody C. *No One's Coming to Save You:*

Navigating Life After Relationship Abuse. North Carolina: CS Publishing, 2025.

5. Holmes, Robert L. et al. *Nonviolence in Theory and Practice.* Illinois: Waveland Press, Inc., 2005.

6. hooks, bell. *All About Love: New Visions.* New York: William Morrow Paperbacks, 2018.

7. hooks, bell. *Rock My Soul: Black People and Self-Esteem.* New York: Atria Books, 2004.

8. Perry, Bruce D. et al. *What Happened to You?: Conversations on Trauma, Resilience, and Healing.* New York: Flatiron Books, 2021.

9. Pratt, Victoria. *The Power of Dignity: How Transforming Justice Can Heal Our Communities.* New York: Seal Press, 2022.

10. Selvaratnam, Tanya. *Assume Nothing: A Story of Intimate Violence.* New York: Harper, 2021.

11. Snyder, Rachel Louise. *No Visible Bruises: What We Don't Know About Domestic Violence Can Kill Us.* New York: Bloomsbury, 2020.

12. Sorrell, Deidra A. *The Black Friendship Project: A Modern Guide to Healthy Friendships.* December 2024.

13. Sow, Aminatou, and Ann Friedman. *Big Friendship: How We Keep Each Other Close.* New York: Simon & Schuster, 2021.

14. Tawwab, Nedra Glover. *Drama Free: A Guide to Managing Unhealthy Family Relationships.* New York: TarcherPerigee, 2023.

15. Tawwab, Nedra Glover. *Set Boundaries, Find Peace: A Guide to Reclaiming Yourself.* New York: TarcherPerigee, 2021.

About the author

Melody Gross is a bold voice, trusted expert, self-proclaimed disruptor, and unwavering advocate for survivors of domestic violence.

Born and raised in Harlem, Melody writes nonfiction that challenges, affirms, and educates. Her work doesn't shy away from the uncomfortable—it leans in with honesty, clarity, and a deep belief in the power of truth. As a survivor herself, she brings both personal insight and professional expertise to the page and speaking engagements, bridging the gap between what survivors actually need and what the world too often fails to provide.

Melody's journey to becoming a speaker and author was born out of necessity. Speaking out saved her, and now, she writes to create pathways for others to feel seen, heard, and supported. Whether she's consulting and training companies through her business Couragoeus SHIFT, leading prevention work through her nonprofit, the Eva Lee Parker Foundation, or mentoring those navigating harm, Melody's message is clear: we all have a role to play in ending intimate partner violence. Her books *No One's Coming to Save You* and *You Can't Save Us* are urgent, raw, and an invitation to listen deeply, act bravely, and remember that healing is possible, even when it's hard.

She now resides in Charlotte, North Carolina, with her talented and funny teenage son. Away from the page and podium, Melody finds joy in decorating her home for Christmas, randomly dancing, singing, or spitting rap lyrics, and exploring all forms that celebrate art, culture, and history. Her life and writing are a testament to resilience—not the polished kind, but the type forged in fire, rooted in community, lit by optimism, and driven by courage.

Endnotes

Family

1. Black, M.C., Basile, K.C., Breiding, M.J., Smith, S.G., Walters, M.L., Merrick, M.T., Chen, J., & Stevens, M.R. (2011). The National Intimate Partner and Sexual Violence Survey (NISVS): 2010 Summary Report. Atlanta, GA: National Center for Injury Prevention and Control, Centers for Disease Control and Prevention. https://www.thehotline.org/stakeholders/domestic-violence-statistics/ 8/5/2025

Friends

1. Fedovskiy, K., Higgins, S., Paranjape, A. (2008). Intimate partner violence: How does it impact major depressive disorder and post-traumatic stress disorder among immigrant Latinas? Journal of Immigrant and Minority Health, 10(1), 45-51. https://www.thehotline.org/stakeholders/domestic-violence-statistics/ 8/5/2025

Neighbors

1. The National Rural Health Association policy brief <u>Rural Community Violence: An Untold Public Health E p i d e m i c</u>. <u>https://www.ruralhealthinfo.org/topics/violence-and -abuse</u> Retrieved 8/5/2025

Employers and Colleagues

1. Domestic violence issues lead to nearly 8 million lost days of paid work each year, the equivalent of over 32,000 full-time jobs.

2. National Institute for Occupational Safety and Health (N I O S H) . https://www.dir.ca.gov/dosh/Workplace-Violence/G eneral-Industry.html

3. Ninety-four percent (94%) of corporate security and safety directors at companies nationwide rank domestic violence as a high-security concern. https://www.congress.gov/bill/110th-congress/senat e-bill/1136/text

4. Costs of Intimate Partner Violence Against Women in the United States Department of Health and Human Services Centers for Disease Control and Prevention National Center for Injury Prevention and Control

5. Society of Human Resources Management (SHRM) https://www.shrm.org/topics-tools/news/risk-management/domestic-violence-comes-to-work

6. Training Magazine. https://trainingmag.com/2023-training-industry-report/

7. Society for Human Resource Management survey. https://www.shrm.org/topics-tools/news/risk-management/domestic-violence-comes-to-work

www.ingramcontent.com/pod-product-compliance
Lightning Source LLC
Chambersburg PA
CBHW051527120626
46551CB00012B/1115